Disposable Camera

T0289331

PHOENIX POETS

JANET FOXMAN

Disposable Camera

THE UNIVERSITY OF CHICAGO PRESS

Chicago & London

JANET FOXMAN is a freelance writer and editor, as well as a senior production editor at a publishing house.

The University of Chicago Press, Chicago 60637
The University of Chicago Press, Ltd., London
© 2012 by Janet Foxman
All rights reserved. Published 2012.
Printed in the United States of America
21 20 19 18 17 16 15 14 13 12   1 2 3 4 5

ISBN-13: 978-0-226-92411-3 (paper)
ISBN-13: 978-0-226-92412-0 (e-book)
ISBN-10: 0-226-92411-4 (paper)
ISBN-10: 0-226-92412-2 (e-book)

Library of Congress Cataloging-in-Publication Data
Foxman, Janet.
    [Poems. Selections]
    Disposable camera / Janet Foxman.
        pages ; cm. — (Phoenix poets)
    Poems.
    Includes bibliographical references.
    ISBN-13: 978-0-226-92411-3 (paperback : alkaline paper)
    ISBN-10: 0-226-92411-4 (paperback : alkaline paper)
    ISBN-13: 978-0-226-92412-0 (e-book)
    ISBN-10: 0-226-92412-2 (e-book)
    I. Title. II. Series: Phoenix poets.
    PS3606.O96D57 2012
    811'.54—dc23   2012017789

Contents

Acknowledgments

My thanks to the editors at *Commonweal*, where "Anagramist's Song" and "Palindromist's Song" first appeared.

To my parents and sisters, Brian Holland, Susie Hwang, Deth Sao, Hiwet Bekele Samimi, Miriam Schiffer, and Chung Won I am inexpressibly indebted. Warmest thanks also to Robert Pinsky; my peers at the Boston University Creative Writing Department—especially Brandy Barents, Matthew Boudway, and Lonnie Manns; and to Randolph Petilos, Susan Karani, and Micah Fehrenbacher at the University of Chicago Press.

Everlasting gratitude to Frank Bidart, from whose discernment and candor these poems benefited from the start; and to Louise Glück, for her inestimable insight and friendship, and for giving this manuscript the most generous scrutiny it could have hoped for.

One

NEW HOUSE

Dad who thinks life is a paper bag
Gets heavier and heavier
You hold until the bottom drops out

Says make me a poem that starts sad
And ends happy
Nobody's ever done that before

He's never read the one about the dead people
Shining in paradise and the light reaching them
Out of colanders almost

Today he says his new house is like being
On vacation every day
That he sleeps like a baby

That the boxwood under his window
Is so pretty you want to pee in your pants
That he is happy all the time

THE ORCHESTRA

For my father

A violinist should always be happy when he is playing.
If he is playing well, he should be happy that he is playing well.
If he is not playing well, he should be happy because it will soon be over.

—Jascha Heifetz

1

The orchestra is a place for perverts—
also for a pimp (the personnel manager),
a Peeping Tom, two bigamists, a pusher
who deals Ecstasy after practice.

The people in the orchestra like
to fuck each other:
in a corner in the pit
a cot for the piccolo and third clarinet,
herpes from the bassoonist to the cellists
then to the tympanist and some violinists, &c.

Complaints from the audience
a bassist is looking down, during concerts,
women's shirts.

2

At the rehearsal for Ravel's *Bolero*—
Berrruuummp berrruuump berrruuump bump bump—
Toscanini, who'd with his stick
poke his concertmaster in the eye, says:

It was magnificent but could you
make a small change.

4

The snare drummer
tries, wants to
please his conductor.
Toscanini stops him again—

the guy's hands shake so much,
his tempo starts
to fall apart.
Toscanini rages,

wants five minutes
later, to fire the guy.
The thing is, it was almost perfect
the first time.

3

*A Musician on Conducting
(Mozart Symphony #40 in G Minor)*

move the stick,   move the stick,   show something—
move the stick,   move the stick,   show nothing—

4

A musician calls the orchestra office asks for the conductor
and is told that he is dead
The musician calls back twenty-five times and gets the same message
I just like to hear you say it he says

5

In the bathroom door
a trick lock:
Heifetz wanted to put them
in their place
early: sent them

to wash their hands
before the first lesson.

6

The Concertmaster Decides to Play the Violin

In the crib trying to compose
The Best Song: his first
memory.

Carries it to the alley and smashes it: his first
violin.

7

People always buy an instrument that's got
the sound they started out with, like a mother.
Start with a crappy instrument, end
with a crappy instrument.

A lady in the orchestra had a cello
with a dark and thuddy sound.
A luthier remade it masterfully,
gave it the tone of the Italian
golden period—*a miracle.*

But a wasted miracle:
to restore the thud right away
the lady restrung it.

8

The look, in the hallway mirror,
of the violin under your ear!
The animals your hand resembled there!
The spiders! The delicate birds!

9

The audience should sit quietly & listen.
It is common courtesy for all concerned to sit quietly.
Audience members should not leave during a performance.
Audience members should bring cough drops
if they have a cough so as to avoid coughing during a performance.
Cough drops should be unwrapped discreetly; rustling paper will disturb
   the performers.
Audience members should not clap between movements.
They should wait until the entire piece is completed before clapping.

10

A conductor and a violist are standing in the middle of the road:
which one do you run over first and why?
The conductor—business before pleasure.

11

The Concertmaster Decides to Leave the Orchestra

They are playing *Carmina Burana*,
so earthy, so infectious,
things in it to put anybody in paradise.
He looks into the audience:
only four people smiling.

12

Nothing much happened but sometimes
people fell out of their chairs playing,
dropped their instruments on stage.
Or strings unwound during concerti.
Once during the *Pathétique*
somebody in the audience died.

When we played beautifully
sometimes they got quiet.

Remember how I played sometimes—
when I had them in my hand:
no coughing.

13

When the music is *beautiful*,
the walls, the hall itself hardly holds together.
You're not sure the roof
won't come off.

The light that turns buildings gold
is pouring in.

14

Why are they clapping?
They thought it was
sad and beautiful?

15

The old Wurlitzer was removed to a roller rink. Every Thursday night an
organist plays wartime music there. Like magnificent birds, chains of men
in velour holding each other at the waist and three women, who were young
when the songs were new, and came here separately, appear untroubled as
they fly, and innocent.

SMORZANDO

Sight reading music a dead man marked—

How itty-bitty the two of us make Mozart!
How Schubert shrinks when we play!

Get it away from me. Get it away.

DECIDING BETWEEN FAR- OR NEAR-SIGHTEDNESS BEFORE EYE SURGERY

He wonders if the sequoia and tea roses
if the mounds the moles have cast
between them, are worth seeing clearly.

He knows he wants to see what could
trip him. He doesn't want to trip.

He wants to know if in the end
it's better to see into the distance.

But whether to see spiders well, the cracks in the wall.
To see, without glasses, the music on the stand.
Or in the middle of the night to not have to ask
what the clock says.

PAGES FROM MY FATHER'S DREAM JOURNAL

Something about a cut on a pocket of a shirt.
Pop is living under the ocean.
He comes to earth.
There is a box with three glasses—dirty.
I don't want him to drink from them.
They might grow the hump on his back.

———

I'm in a closet.
I don't understand what I did wrong.
They have glued wallpaper around the edges.
It's pretty but it's not on tight.
I say: I think this could be fixed up a little.

———

I'm kissing and hugging Osama bin Laden.
There's a cut halfway under his eye.
I'm thanking him for not destroying all the carpet
when he robbed my mother's house.
She loves him for stealing just part of it so neatly.
I'm waiting to get packages of food out of the car.
My mother is there.
She's holding an old thank you card (for flowers).
I tear it up.
One package is empty.
The other I put on the backseat where Whoopie is tied up.
We drive past the house on Pico where God lived.

———

I'm sitting at a restaurant.
They're serving unfinished portions of people's food.
Fish pancakes? I don't want to eat here.
There is oil on the table.
One of my daughters puts her sleeve in the oil.
(I don't think she notices.)
She has on the sweater I gave her.

———

I'm standing in line to buy meatballs in a butcher shop.
I'm buying the cheapest.
The best is made of goat.
Whoopie is in the other room.
There is a contest on TV.
I want her to come to me.
But the flies on my face are keeping me company.

———

Something about me playing a bow.
The Metropole Orchestra outside before a performance.
Two or three young men and a female concertmaster.
One of the young men has thinning hair.
I have played my bow for Susan.
She has heard another,
but she says mine is full of subtlety
and the other just overwhelms her with sound.

———

I'm in a city I don't know,
a long time ago.
We're walking along and Susan says I have something

in the crease of my nose.
I pull at it. It's like clay—loose.
I put it in my pocket and think This is what death is made of.

—

A story about three men—
one who's going to die.
One is going to be caught and die by an insect.
There is no way of stopping the story or the death.

—

I'm explaining to Darlene that the last notes of the Chausson *Poème* were so
difficult that even if I could play it, it wouldn't do any good.

—

His little dog comes back to a place
where other dogs are waiting, mostly in pairs.
One of them looks like him so he kicks it twice.

—

Susan and I are discussing what to do during an earthquake.
We are living at an old folks' home.
There's a window to the left and a stair to the right,
an extra support to the right of her bed.
There's a bull hanging from the ceiling
whistling a requiem to God.

—

Twenty-eight wedges of cake on a shelf,
each representing seven or fifteen hours of happiness.

—

Many cars going downhill. Passing me narrowly,
narrowly missing accidents.
Finally somebody is hit.
I'm with people.
I meet Myra Kestenbaum. She looks beautiful.
She gives me opuses of Grieg, Beethoven.
I am willing to learn everything.

SOUVENIR

And those stars trembling under the Coliseum's dome
during the ice show?

Light sabers, fiber-optic wands—
children contented at the souvenir stands in the lobby.

How did they come to light
so numerously, and so suddenly?

A man's voice, or Mickey Mouse's,
cooed an order over the loudspeaker.
Or somebody in the control room dimmed the lights.

And those hasty nebulas emitting stars whenever they stopped?

Vendors climbing the stairs along the bleachers.

In the box seats—the Pleiades?
That globular cluster?

A girl's birthday party;
an only child.

The black matter between?

Funded this heaven—but afraid.
Afraid its hold on any of the constituent stars
is as loose as its hold on those impersonal ones
that pass over the houses they share with these.

What happened?

The melodrama began on the ice under us.
The maid figure-eighted out of a florescent forest,
mimed an apostrophe to a mirror, or a wishing well made of cardboard.
All along, the prerecorded bleating of monarchs and dogs.

THREE PICTURES

PUBLIC GARDEN

Birds. Hey birds! birds!
They don't even know me, the birds.
Then crying.

CEMETERY

Aldan! All din!—
Baby's first word.
All done, all done—the name
of her brother roller skating
down a path too far from her.

FAIR

The youngest one lifted onto
a pony for the first time—
a wail impossible
for our alphabet to imitate—
being monosyllabic, like a body bag.

FERRYBOAT

A woman is telling her husband the sun
looks like diamonds where it
touches the water.
Like thousands of diamonds—
and she begins to count them—

One of those days, in other words,
when looking at water feels peaceful.

———

This *is* peaceful.
This is *peaceful.*

———

Cupolas. Empty porches and gazebos.
Shuttered windows toward the sea; or in the arched
windows of houses near the tabernacle— NO TRESPASSING.
Beauty nobody gets to have when they're
not here, but that is theirs.

———

Above the sea
a bird heaves itself
toward the dark.

———

Crossing the sound,
such envy of birds
from my bench on the boat.

POSTCARD FROM MY HOMETOWN IN SUMMER

The people are so happy here!
They walk barefoot alongside big American dogs.
They smile without embarrassment when they hand off restroom keys at
open-air cafés.

Were they always this happy?
Every year, a parade down Broadway, a fair on the waterfront—
Remind me. Was that an ostrich or a prostrate lion we rode?
All I remember is the merry-go-round,
the itinerant rides blinking like a street of jewelry shops.

DISPOSABLE CAMERA

For Karen

To a disposable camera I have confined the paradise
where my sister lives—

palisades, sycamores. Sunbathers mistaken for statuary.
People with shears, shrubbery cut into sea creatures.

Lemon trees bloom in front of houses.
Trophy wives escort children through mazes of palm trees.

In the shadows of palms the children paw their toys delicately
while the youngest one rides his plastic motorcycle toward his mother

with a confidence so absolute, so heartbreakingly
beautiful, everybody at the pier

hopes nothing will ever humiliate it, that it will persist
after the camera runs out of film.

Two

PALINDROMIST'S SONG

Was it a rat I saw?
Was it a car or a cat I saw?

Was it a bat I saw?

I did. Did I?

God! A wasp saw a dog.
Oh who was it I saw? Oh, who.

SEVEN WAYS OF PARAPHRASE

Only for the limp rally of paraphrase
wave your banners of flesh.

See that hissing tree, with the brown leaves still holding on—
I am its paraphrase.

The sweet paraphrase of your sweet arms:
the Notdespitebutbecause, which is love.

With the minutiae of paraphrase our mirrors
mock us.

That to paraphrase even God must stoop
the burning bush was proof.

A small orange fire
is paraphrase for *woman smoking at night.*

A struck stone wishes it were Pegasus and is
his paraphrase.

LETTERS TO MY TWIN

1

In our double stroller past our first birthday—
that picture of us at the pumpkin patch.
You looked like me—
but in your bonnet, also like a tulip
and (your arms) a pterodactyl.

2

Doctors were stitching Siamese
twins back together—

redoubling, pro bono, hearts and lungs.
I told the nurses we'd been born

stuck together.

REPLICA APPENDAGE SIDESHOW YOUR SELF

I am what I think you think I am

SIDESHOW APPENDAGE

3

A funny word, *pear.*
                    Pare in it.
                              And *reap.*

Likewise *pair.*
                Air in it.
                          And *rip.*

4

As fast as he could Nigidius marked a potter's wheel
twice with ink—*so that the strokes* (Augustine tells us)

seemed to fall on the very same part of it.

For a twin being born each stroke would stand—

the space between *equivalent to the revolution*
in the celestial sphere accounting for their separate fates.

Upon the rim of the wheel—
the marks, at no small distance apart.

5

Noes sonnes and Noes wyfe and the wyues of his sonnes
Wyth them in to the arke:

They and all maner of beastes in their kynde
And all maner of wormes that crepe vppon the erth in their kynde

And all maner of byrdes in there kynde.
And all maner off foules what soever had feders.

And they came vnto Noe in to the arke by cooples
Of all flesh yt had breth of lyfe in it.

And the floud came .xl. dayes and .xl. nyghtes vppon the erth
And the water increased and bare vp the arcke

And it was lifte vp from of the erth
And the water prevayled and increased exceadingly vppon the erth:

And all fleshe that moved on the erth bothe birdes catell and beastes
Perisshed with al that crepte on the erth and all men.

6

The wife reciting the deepest things she
confessed to a diary:

The camera pans out—
the husband asleep on the sofa.

Then: divorced for seven years they are holding
each other in a bed in a cabin in the Swedish countryside.

7

Your letter:

The barber was blowdrying his own hair when I passed the shop today.
In the mirror he was admiring himself!

Are barbers supposed to do that?

xo,

Laura

8

Two brothers named Jim were adopted by different families.
Before they knew anything about each other:

Each Jim married a woman named Betty!

Each Jim divorced Betty & married a woman named Linda!

Each Jim got in the habit of flushing the toilet before he takes a shit!

Each Jim built a white bench around a tree in his yard!

9

I never realize until I get
to the register:

2 buttermilks
2 baskets of Turkish figs
2 sole fillets

10

to to to to to to
two two two two two two
too too too too too too
2 2 2 2 2 2
tu tu tu tu tu tu

11

Many entire strangers are more like them than they are like each other,
though separated at birth by the smallest interval of time, [and] at conception
generated by the same act of copulation, and at the same moment.
—Saint Augustine, *The City of God*

12

Grammar Duet: The Conjunction Symphony

FIRST MOVEMENT

Twin 1: *We is.*
Twin 2: *We is.*

SECOND MOVEMENT

Twin 1: *I am.*
Twin 2: *We is (isn't we?).*

THIRD MOVEMENT

Twin 1: *I am.*

Twin 2: *You are; I was.*

FOURTH MOVEMENT

Twin 1: *I am.*

Twin 2: *I am too—if I have to be.*

ENCORE (in the event of a standing ovation)

Twin 1: *I am.*

Twin 2: *I am.*

13

Pairs of twins were asked if they had engaged in the following activities *frequently, occasionally,* or *not at all* during the past year:

Went ice skating. Took cough syrup.
Cared for tropical or goldfish. Shot a gun.
Took a sleeping pill. Sang in a church choir.
Attended a burlesque show. Went square dancing.
Cared for a potted plant. Took tranquillizing pills.
Read the Bible. Danced the Twist.
Participated in a drag race. Took a laxative.
Twirled a baton. Took Aspirin.
Read poetry that was not required reading. Discussed sexual matters with
    your mother.
Discussed sexual matters with your father. Discussed sexual matters with a
    male friend.
Discussed sexual matters with a female friend. Used a thermometer to take
    your temperature.
Attended a religious revival meeting. Wore sunglasses after dark.
Ate a steak cooked rare. Visited a friend's home overnight.

Had a friend visit your home overnight. Had your back rubbed.
Tried to hypnotize somebody. Taught Sunday school.
Cried. Kissed your mother.
Kissed your father. Hit or slapped a boy of your own age.
Hit or slapped a girl of your own age. Was hit or slapped by a girl of your own age.
Was hit or slapped by a boy of your own age. Collected insect specimens.
Rode a horse. Obtained the autograph of a famous person.
Had a quarrel with your twin. Confused people by pretending to be your twin.
Ate candy. Cut your own hair.

14

The days
I am happy
people tell me
I look
like you.

15

Paradise & The Ascension.

The Annunciation & The Presentation.

The Child & The Crucifixion—

                        Time across a diptych.

The Flagellation

            (that prancing around the pole with whips like articulate eels,
            the painter's relish in the folds of those auburn silks)—

MOUTHS: IN THEIR OWN WORDS

Gum Chewer

> Xyllilphl phfllul phchlylhiul
> hubba bubba.

My Dad's Mouth

> WHAT in t h e
> HELL?

Joey Buttafuoco's Wife's Mouth

> I got crooked
> when she got shot.

Phone Sex Operator's Mouth

> Pussy and cock
> just roll off the tongue.

Sick Person's Mouth

> O my God, I say,
> when the head I live in turns green.

SWIMMERS

In the distance
a pink thing made a V on the water
and a little fountain spurted from it:

the pink was
an arm and the fountain
was legs kicking.

It was a pink fish
made of human.
Then something amazing:

another pink fish! Alongside
his yellow dog
swam a man, grand

like a travertine statue of a man.
Then swans,
and three swimming heads.

It was the kind of scene that
restores in its viewers a belief
in the terrestrial perfection of things.

EVENING POEM

Lights are on
inside houses.
People holding remote controls or phones.
You can just see the midsections

of the people, the houses seem
so flat.
A smear of white limos and ugly flowers—
meant to tease the virginity out

of somebody—eclipses
the entrance lobby
of the Holiday Inn.
Against a wall

a sober man pisses,
while out of a bar
drunk men bloom.
Faint disclosures fall

between trees.
Inside, the regulars
are asking girls if they could
please squeeze

their titties and would they
like some fine black bone?
Far away, the 6:14 crosses the aqueduct
toward a compounding quiet.

The air inside the train
is dark and ceremonious,
as if the night had been inlaid
with otter teeth or carved

from whale bone.
There is a woman by whose porcine legs
you can tell she used
to be a dancer.

No longer do they look
capable of kicking
up cumbrous
puffy skirts.

LAST ACT: THE CREATION

A man in a cloth diaper crosses
the stage to tell the setting.
Out again comes the famous mime.

All that illegible gesticulating—
what is he, God?

No. Only a man in a white unitard waving his hands
through puffs of dry ice—a dead art.

Three

REX

Three times a day
the woman next door is pulled across

our living room window by her dog, whose life is tripartite:
Piss against a bush. Crap between tall grass. Sniff ass.

She is happy to let her dog
shit on our tree.

Her son's name is Rex
and he climbs the gray branches

of his mother's magnolia and caws at passersby.
He is a funny bird up there

and nobody likes him.
He spits on the neighbors

and pounds on his head while he rocks back
and forth. When the ice cream truck

comes singing down our street
he runs after it flapping his arms

and the dog runs after him
but with no arms to flap.

JELLYFISH

You probably think things are worth
doing. You probably think people should go on
having babies. You probably think people will care
about those babies after they're born.

I bet you feel sad when you see birds dying.
I bet you look up at the sky some days
and think, Oh how pretty.

I know your type.
You use old-fashioned words like *dignity*;
you call lust *yearning*.
You probably think *orifice* refers to the constellation
with the hunter holding a club.

Haven't you seen the medusa swimming?
That yielding riot of tentacles bringing plankton
to the mouth in the bell?
Then the venomous flinging of the barbed stingers?
Those nasty and glorious, magnificent stingers!
Incorporating the sea that streams around it,
its weight—

And the translucences and streaks of translucences
blooming in the Bay of Biscay!
Inside the jellyfish's clear, membranous cup—
the salmon florescences ringing!

And yet, you prefer the polyp.
The impotent stalk that eats only when food happens by.

And you like your poets to pass
by lamp-lit windows with people in them
and to think about those people
but not get an erection thinking about them.

DUBUFFET ON UNCERTAINTY

I   FEMME ENTRE DEUX HOMMES (GOUACHE)

For the pale apple of your body
Which out of your waist erupts, their tongues stiffen,
And their terrier hands—one from each of them—try to sculpt or hold you down.

You say: I lost my arms.

Wipe off that idiot smile, the happy crescents
That have risen across your face! They're reaching through you, past
The apple, for the maple trees of each other.

You say: I lost my arms.

2   SITUATIONS INCERTAINES
(ACRYLIC AND PAPER COLLAGE ON CANVAS)

Here uncertainty is
a bubble
or coffin
or bed

whose dark lineaments adhere like fact.
It is a dermal adumbration that almost tells the truth.

The rubber impossibility of our impetuous feet,
the feebleness to enfold anything—

we sigh
or die
or fly
in epigrams of gold that impersonate the city, city at night.

Whether or not the confusion of the world and a dog
are intended is hard to tell;
into the stippled ground that spills illegibly
at your feet, spiders and claws and asterisks
are darkly woven, and then taper off. This nervous textile
might be an audience.

See all those places where flicks refrain—
they could be mouths
gasping. They could be
a rapt audience in profile.

Oxymoron and ambush overhang the handiwork
at your feet, which could be a human audience;
the bastard wings of the violin's descant
squirm against each other and like locusts
darken the air.

You wonder for whom you tell your body
to flit; does anybody hear
you? Or is it
all just the otiose warble of cow guts and horsehair?

The awkward gallop of my old limbs in the audience's stare.
My life has died like eighth notes on the air.

The dog stands on its hind legs and listens.
Listen: the dog stands on its hind legs.

LETTER

Tonight I sat at one of the tables on the carousel side of the park.
The picnics, the featheriness of dresses in the middle ground—
Breathtaking. Breathtaking, the people at peace further off under
    the cooling trees.

A ring of women with unfinished flowers in their laps
Had formed near the center of the grass.
Beside each woman, a mound of pale thread that diminished

Negligibly with each stitch that brought her flower closer to blooming.
Against the elms the sun was setting too high
To admit even one of these needleworkers.

Suddenly from elsewhere on the grass an exhilarated yelp.
He was pinning her down!
And she was squirming to get free and she got free and pinned him down!

Then under her he was squirming!
I thought of you. And craved to pin you down.
And craved for you to pin me down.

It was getting dark.
The happy wrestlers got up and left.

In the lighted windows of the wholesale shops,
Stuffed animals bearing hearts, and music boxes,
And other tokens of love that can be had there only by the dozen.

I thought of the twelve chenille birds I bought for you.
How you wrapped the claws
Of the two you spared around the lamp at your bed.

DINNER À DEUX

On his bedroom floor I ate
Falafel from the bowl

He held between us
And from his hand

My portion of a bird's nest
And a date mamool

Then from the takeout bag
That seemed to intuit

My gratitude
With its rows of THANK YOUS

He took a napkin
And there transliterated

My name into
His native language

And mercifully didn't wipe
His mouth with it

LINES FOR A LOVE POEM

A hand working a rag against
The window from outside

A hand working a rag against
The window from inside

Each had had enough of seeing
The world through dirt

NEW LIFE

1

Under the oaks, raccoons gorge
on apricots. Pines focus their sugar

into cones. And the mountain—
a piece of ice—magnificent—

and happy to be so much in the middle
of nature. Even the spiders are better here.

Yesterday two of them divided
above the pantry door and crawled

along the ceiling away
from each other, until they joined

their matching arcs above the stove.
Such endearing little things,

and generous to let themselves be
crushed elsewhere than the freshly painted walls.

2

In the city where I was a girl,
new sunken gardens.
New glass buildings with penthouses.
Chocolatiers instead of candy shops.

When did the sister cities gift
the granite dragons? The mammoth
bronzes for which these new pagodas?

The Joan of Arc at Glisan & 39th—
her spear, all the muscles in the horse
under her—regilded.

Yesterday a barista (one of that new species)
did something I'd never seen anywhere—
with froth made a feather in my cup,
a milk heart in yours.

3

New Year's at the bar under the bridge.
Young couples drunk on Satans
feed each other tiny chocolate cakes dusted with gold.

That was the week the piano tuner died.
At the cathedral where the freeway cloverleafs
five choirs console the air in eulogy to him.

4

In the hills above Front Avenue the forest began.
To the right, cargo ships and cranes.
If Toyotas across the river gleamed
where barges delivered them
there was sun.

On the way home, terrific calm
if it was evening
and a factory's side door was open
and a welder was torching things together—

The road ended in a refinery,
eventually a bridge to an island.

5

Sick of regretting that we trained the wisteria up rather than through
   the pergola.
Sick of the door opening onto the same cramped hallway.
Sick of those peach shuttered rooms.

So what if the new owners paper over the birds in the master bedroom.
So what if they like the garden well enough to learn the common name
   for *dicentra*.

6

Plum crumble with our new neighbors.
Tribes used to chase elk off the cliff
our houses share. Used to eat meat
where they fell.

7

A wedding party crowds the hollow
in the sandblasted basalt—
the grotto's pietà at the center of their half circle.

The neighbor to the north said her house is full of honey—hundreds of
pounds of honey. The bees have been gone fifteen years, but sometimes their
fumigated sugar seeps from the vacant combs through cracks in the stucco.

8

What about the wool flowers hanging
in their Victorian shadow box unsettles you?

Do they remind you too much
of our daughters?

9

The mountain turns
pink before it disappears.

You light a fire.

In the molded panels flanking the new fireplace,

that silkscreen insisting in oranges and purples and a font
decades out-of-date

NEW LIFE NEW LIFE NEW LIFE.
The woodcut of a moon over conjoined firs—

SPRING
After The Marketplace

Before the child went to buy naan
he set down his potted geranium.

He rushed through the scalloped shade of vendors' tarps
all the way from the bread stall—but the flower was gone.

Have you seen a beam of light with a flower in it?
The people shaking their heads no made him tearful.

Only the girl in the fruit stand knew where his flower was:
The light had moved, but not the clay ledge where he left it.

Four

CHRIST'S ENTRY INTO BRUSSELS (ENSOR)

It must be the Jubilee:
the vagueeyed goldmedallioned band plays its brassy song, fancy hats
curl into glad pink erections, and from balconies heads
expunge purple cataracts.

At the center of this festive horde of assorted pleasureseekers and human beasts
perfection, i.e. Jesus, waves
an affectionate, steady hand from the back of a byzantine ass.

THE FÜHRER DESCENDS FROM HEAVEN (OR THE FIRST TWENTY MINUTES OF *TRIUMPH OF THE WILL*)

The Führer has chosen the best place on earth
To drop down on. All the people are waving to him,
And the voluptuous women are pointing at him.
There are white linen handkerchiefs and window boxes too.

Across the crowd—
A blur of salutation and desire—
The Führer's right hand goes up,
Luminous and birdlike.

The Führer passes under
A bannered bridge and then the world opens up to him again
In a bright circle with row houses and people and garlands inside. A mother
    and child break
From the crowd to give him a bouquet; how lovely.

Then the Führer cocks his head a little
To watch hanging banners twist like ribbons.
He looks at the banners so delicately,
He must have a poetic eye.

Night falls.
The Führer stands at the belvedere.
Torches light the place, pretty
Like fireflies.

Then day breaks in an army camp.
There are tents and tepees and men there.
The men part each other's hair and wash each other's backs.
Then they carry a wagon of wood

To the kitchen. The chef looks like a beautiful king,
And he cooks sausages.
The army men wrestle, and above a trampoline
A boy scrambles in the air.

Then the parade again.
A girl eats an apple, and the Führer appears.
A boy sucks his fingers, and the Führer appears.
And some of the women lick their lips.

MASACCIO ADDRESSES EVE AT
THE BRANCACCI CHAPEL

For each other, from the opposite cages
into which your nose's impassable bridge has stranded them,
the dark birds of your eyes invent dirges—

Each note like a bow on ten thousand strings at once;
in an instant, nomenclature for every species of grief—

Your brown mouth opens like a nest
to save them, but the sadness that was almost already there flies
out like a stream of sparrows from a moldering chimney, and has already
    hatched its eggs.

ANAGRAMIST'S SONG

Notes, stone.
A spider, despair.

Garden?
Danger.

Eucharist?
Ah curse it!

Desperation—
A rope ends it.

HARVEST FAIR

Three women with home perms adjudicate
Jars of honey in a glass-sealed room

The balloon man asks what animal I want
I tell him the snake the tree the hand

He did the Statue of Liberty once
But it would take too long four hours maybe

So he makes instead a translucent horse
And from the same balloon presses a baby into it

Hard to do he says handing it to me

THE PAUSE (TILO BAUMGÄRTEL)

For Sunje

The dahlias in glass vases at the tearoom in Suzhou.
The duck with the Ming emperor's profile
hanging in a window by the gate downtown.
The people were a bouquet repeating the reflection of the people on the water—
You might describe the crowd that gathered in Datong
for the Ceremony of the Dead.
So many images for the love letters you would write
once you mastered this script!

———

The scribe who bequeathed his craft to you
sees the brush stop above the character
that has already stuttered six times across your page.

———

Like a squid he withdrew.
The page disappeared in a blot of ink.

———

Do the images now seem irredeemably modest,
impotent like the dragon that goes down
Jinan Street at the New Year?

Is this why your pity for the crabs huddled
into the corners of tanks at the restaurant
where you eat watercress and pastries filled
with red-bean paste
deepens into inconsolable dread?

———

You asked to know the character for *human being*.
The scribe drew a wishbone.
It looks like two people leaning into each other he said.

LOVE POEM

You were a faux-bois
bath,
then a feeder
filled
with thistle
seed & safflower,
then the dearest
branch.

Into countable
birds
my heart
exploded—
into quenchless
birds
who cooled
& perched & ate.

HERMIT'S GLOSSARY

ART

Best (for the cloth's sake) to boil or pierce them and unravel the cocoon in
  one continuous thread.

BOYHOOD

Quite something, in hide-and-seek, being sought.
Quite something, hiding.

Loving best birds and worms
I climbed trees,
dug toward the center of the earth with twigs.

Quite something (in Red Rover) being called for
across the grass. I learned to love
my name breaking
through or getting caught in the chain.

CELIBACY

If I were a worm I would proliferate
by fragmentation.

DISGUST (OF THE SELF)

Why this fly settling
next to me?

I'm sure he isn't well;
he won't be scared away.

EXULTATION

Those yellow spontaneous fountains amid the grazing asses.

FELLOWSHIP

Ivory, tortoiseshell, horsehair—
in one cello bow, such harmony among species.

GUILT

On a path to the monument opposite
the harbor islands

seven boys stood in a ring: a bird was dying.
Is he dying. Is he dying—

In the distance, pleasure boats were passing.
The tiny wet eye was blinking and blinking.

Heartbreaking they were
addressing me.

HOME

Oh uncared for fish!
Feeding on the water you shit in!

IRRELEVANCE

Within their own lacework spiders dying.

JUSTICE

The pit that claimed more coyotes than cats.
The remains of predators outnumbering the remains of prey.

KNOWLEDGE

Into a bucket one August
a magician dumped popcorn and pulled out
a rabbit.
All the children in the park lined
up to pet it.

Impassively or softly, or violently to confirm reality—
how variously the convoy of small hands
touched it!
The guiltless rapture of the smallest hands,
nothing sweeter in the world.

I looked down at my own hand.
My hand was dirty now—
no fountain, no sink
close enough to get it clean.

LONELINESS

In a field the color of a camel,
a camel all by itself in a field.

MEMORY

Into the grotto's rocks gray birds disappearing.

NATURAL DISPOSITION

I poured the fighting fish in together—
foolish test of faith.

One pressed circles against the glass.
The other jabbed, and jabbed from the center of those circles to bite.

There was a blur of fins and color and the water splashed.
A blur of fins and color and the water splashed.

Then to rebuke my hope the water
didn't splash—the achieved solitude of the fighting fish,

to rebuke my hope.

OLD AGE

I told myself that mine was the caterpillar's
indentured servitude to night,
that the heart I was keeping from breaking
was not already broken,
that forbearance would bear me to life.

To love as to the mouth of a cave
forbearance would bear me.
To happiness, then to dignity,
it would bear me.

PARENTHOOD

River, forgive the salmon for conferring custody.
She is trying to keep her grief from being too numerous.

QUIET

Praise to the bowerbird!
Wooing by architecture
not by song.

RECIPROCITY

The sea anemone contracts
however you touch it.

SUMMER

On the other side of a hedge we'd find a hole in
there was always a house.
If we were lucky, a house with a swing,
which meant children lived there.

And the animal whose achievement
was the hole?
It let us see further but kept itself
out of sight until such time as nature
repossessed the tiny passages.

TRUST

Shame on you to test,
after throwing crumbs,
the bird's credulity
with stones.

ULULATION

To miniaturize what it hurt to see
we climbed the cemetery's tower.
The tiny obelisks and endowed shrubs.
The tiny mausoleums and statues of men.
The tiny family plots, like mouths and mouths of loose teeth.

The shadow I cast on the top of an elm
was smaller than yours.
A noise that knew my heart
better than anybody echoed up to us.

A dirty spot that was probably a swan
was tracing invisible circles on the pond.

VESTIGE

The squirrel doesn't know his passion
to gather is panic not hope.

WAKEFULNESS

So much fellow feeling after midnight—
with roaches? mice?

Not in retort but in rephrase the wind
takes the leaves
away: *Everybody needs nobody.*

X-RAY

The pentimenti show the Old Master
painted a tulip open
to inter a portrait of a fly.

YOUTH

Tell me, woodlouse, after you uncurl
to find your rock again.
Speak to tell me life gets better than this.

ZOO

A cage circumscribing every animal,
no wonder a child stuck
his hand into a turnstile
to feed a man a piece of bread.

TABLEAU

From the stairs that spill shadowlessly
Past the esplanade, a woman is framing her lover
In the eye of a camera.

For a few very long minutes the fate of the world
Seems to teeter on this tender undertaking,
And the only thing moving is the adoring glance

That flies between them
Like the birds that will resume flight
Once she's gotten the picture right.

The fullness that picture will commemorate
Is so natural it looks otherworldly—

From the lover's side a stranger enters
To spoil the frame and startle the image back into real time.

In ones and twos toward the metal benches
And willows by the river
The people looking on disband.

Notes

"The Orchestra": I quote from a compilation of musicians' jokes in sections 4 and 10; I quote from a music teacher's rules of etiquette in section 9.

"Palindromist's Song" is an arrangement of found lines.

"Letters to My Twin": Section 5 is from the Tyndale Bible; section 13 is a compression of a list cited in John Loehlin and Robert Nichols's *Heredity, Environment, and Personality: A Study of 850 Sets of Twins* (Austin: University of Texas Press, 1976).